VICTORIA JUSTICE

GET THE SCOOP

unauthorized biography by Ronny Bloom

S0-AFI-076

PSSI
PRICE STERN SLOAN

PRICE STERN SLOAN
Published by the Penguin Group
Penguin Group (USA) Inc., 375 Hudson Street, New York, New York 10014, USA
Penguin Group (Canada), 90 Eglinton Avenue East, Suite 700,
Toronto, Ontario M4P 2Y3, Canada
(a division of Pearson Penguin Canada Inc.)
Penguin Books Ltd., 80 Strand, London WC2R 0RL, England
Penguin Group Ireland, 25 St. Stephen's Green, Dublin 2, Ireland
(a division of Penguin Books Ltd.)
Penguin Group (Australia), 250 Camberwell Road, Camberwell, Victoria 3124, Australia
(a division of Pearson Australia Group Pty. Ltd.)
Penguin Books India Pvt. Ltd., 11 Community Centre, Panchsheel Park,
New Delhi—110 017, India
Penguin Group (NZ), 67 Apollo Drive, Rosedale, North Shore 0632, New Zealand
(a division of Pearson New Zealand Ltd.)
Penguin Books (South Africa) (Pty.) Ltd., 24 Sturdee Avenue,
Rosebank, Johannesburg 2196, South Africa

Penguin Books Ltd., Registered Offices: 80 Strand, London WC2R 0RL, England

Photo credits: Cover: Alberto E. Rodriguez/Getty Images; Insert photos: first page
courtesy of Frank Micelotta/Getty Images; second page courtesy of Charley
Gallay/WireImage; Jeff Vespa/WireImage; third page courtesy of Alexandra
Wyman/WireImage; Chris Hatcher/Prphotos.com; fourth page courtesy of
Kevin Winter/Getty Images; Kevin Mazur/WireImage.

Library of Congress Cataloging-in-Publication Data is available.

ISBN 978-0-8431-9976-5   10 9 8 7 6 5 4 3 2 1

CONTENTS

INTRODUCTION

The room is a studio, wide and spacious. It's also largely empty of furniture. The tall windows would let in plenty of sunlight—if their blinds hadn't been pulled down. For now, all the light is coming from an array of enormous floor lamps, all trained toward the far end of the room. A single figure stands before them, her back to the wall.

Young and slender, she wears a Pucci/No Way Vintage dress. Its long sleeves and high neck contrast with the mid-thigh hem, and the entire thing is scallop-patterned in cream, yellow, pink, and brown. Her long, brown hair has been pulled back around her face but hangs loose below, cascading around her neck and over her collarbone. Large, orange hoop earrings dangle from her ears. A pair of black, open-toed pumps and a vintage ring complete the look. She is a vision of vintage splendor.

A photographer prances around just in front of the lights, snapping shots. He calls out instructions: "Head up! Give us a peace sign! Show me some attitude!" But very little is necessary. The model is a natural. She gives off an energy, an enthusiasm, a charm that easily shows even through these still photos, giving them life and warmth.

That's no surprise, though. After all, Victoria Justice is far more than a model. She's an actress and a singer, and she's used to moving in front of the cameras, portraying a range of characters and emotions. Her cheerful nature and youthful energy can be seen both on and off camera, whether she's posing for pictures or giving an interview.

And she's had lots of experience at posing. Though only sixteen, Victoria is already a famous model. She's been in worldwide ad campaigns for major brands, like GUESS Jeans and Ralph Lauren. Right now she's doing a photo shoot for a feature in *Supermodels Unlimited* magazine, the bi-weekly magazine that focuses on the beauty industry.

Victoria does several more poses, and changes outfits three times: once to a sleeveless, word-patterned, white dress from No Way Vintage and a bulky gold necklace from Metro Retro Vintage; once to a black dress with a bold yellow, orange, and blue pattern from Louis Féraud/No Way Vintage and a cute, black hat from Arturo Rios; and finally to a simple, hot pink dress with thick, black neck straps from Pink Polka Dot, along with a silver and black onyx bracelet and black-and-white polka dot hoop earrings from Zad. She takes time to sit down and do an interview with Renee Shafii, who's impressed by the young model-actress: ". . . I now know what makes Victoria so unbelievably special," Shafii starts the feature. "Her outstanding morals and positive personality."

Then the shoot is finished. Victoria changes back into her own clothes—she tends to favor a more casual look for herself, with Converse sneakers and comfortable clothes, though she does love earrings. "I like to feel laid-back and comfortable in my clothes," she once told *Twist* magazine. "But I like funky too. I dress with my mood!"

Her mom has been there the entire time, and now she whisks Victoria away—to school. That's one of the things that makes Victoria different from most other models and actresses, including those her own age. She's been in several movies, she was a co-star on a hit Nickelodeon series for three years, has done commercials and ad campaigns for major companies, and has even recorded a movie soundtrack—and yet in many ways, she's still a normal teenager. She goes to school rather than being home schooled like many other actors. She has friends outside the entertainment industry. She lives at home with her mother, stepfather, and little sister. She loves to go shopping, hang out with friends, and just kick back and relax and play with her dog.

Victoria is a regular girl, the kind of girl you can talk to and laugh with and have fun hanging out with. At the same time, she's well on her way to becoming world-famous for acting, singing, and modeling. Beautiful but approachable, talented but friendly, professional but down-to-earth—it's no wonder everyone loves Victoria Justice!

CHAPTER 1
PISCES BY A NOSE

Some people find they're drawn to Hollywood. Others are simply born there!

Victoria Dawn Justice was the latter. She was born in Hollywood, all right—Hollywood, Florida! Founded in 1925, the city is one of the largest in the South Florida metropolitan area and borders the Atlantic Ocean. It's not far from Fort Lauderdale (to its north) and Miami (to its south). Victoria was born on February 19, 1993, to Zack and Serene Justice. That means she's a Pisces, but only barely—if she was born just one day earlier, she would have been an Aquarius instead! Because she was born on the edge of two different star signs, astrologists would say Victoria has both Aquarian and Pisces traits. Aquarians are visionaries—they're also independent, witty, well-spoken, playful people who like to experience new things. Pisces are intuitive, sensitive people who use their creativity to inspire others. Sounds like the perfect combination for an actress and model!

Victoria combines more than just star signs—her mother Serene is Puerto Rican and her father Zack is Irish, German, French, and English. This explains Victoria's unique, dark-haired, dark-eyed good looks! And no, she doesn't speak Spanish—"I cannot understand it or speak it," she admitted on her blog, "but would love to have time to learn one day. My great grandparents on my mom's side were born in [Puerto Rico] and my mom can understand everything, and speaks enough to get by."

Both of Victoria's parents loved her a lot, but unfortunately, that wasn't enough to keep their marriage together. Serene and Zack divorced when Victoria was only a year or two old. Victoria's cheerful disposition carried her through the tough time, however, and a little while later, her mom met, fell in love with, and married a man named Mark Reed. Madison Reed, Victoria's half sister, was born in 1996.

Victoria's outgoing nature manifested early.

"I've always kind of been a performer," she told justjaredjr.buzznet.com. "When I was little, I was the kid that made her entire family sit on the couch while I was dressed up and sang all my Barney songs." Even when she was little, Victoria's family and friends knew she was going to be a star! And it was clear that she loved to entertain people.

Hollywood, Florida, was a nice place to grow up. It was big enough to have everything a young girl needed—including malls, movie theaters, good schools, plenty to do, and a five-mile stretch of beach—yet it was still warm and sunny and friendly. Okay, maybe a little too warm and sunny. "Hollywood, Florida is awesome," Victoria told *Girl's Life* magazine during an interview, "but it's really humid and extremely hot." Still, it had its strong points, like sunny skies and nearby beaches. And most of all, it had Victoria's family (other than her dad, who had moved north, to South Carolina). The person Victoria was most grateful to have nearby was probably her mom. "I love my mom," she told starscoop.com. "She's always there with me and everything." It's her mom that Victoria credits for her own levelheaded nature.

That doesn't mean Victoria didn't have dreams, of course. She did—and most of them involved performing! So what happens when you combine a love of entertaining, a desire to perform, and a smart, practical girl? You get Victoria Justice, and a career that started early and has kept growing ever since!

CHAPTER 2
THE FACE OF OVALTINE

At eight years old, most boys and girls are busy learning math and English in school, running around the playground, and playing with their friends. They watch a lot of television, usually cartoons and other kids' shows. Advertisers know their target audience, so the ads they run during those shows have kids, too. The idea is that kids watching will think, "Hey, that kid's my age and has this drink or that snack or those toys. I want those, too!" And it works. Most kids identify with the kids they see on those commercials. Some might look at them and think, "Wow, that's cool that they get to be on TV like that!" A few may even say, "I wish I could do that!" But how many actually get beyond that idle notion?

Victoria certainly did! "I was eight years old," she recounted to *Scholastic* magazine, "and was watching some kid on a commercial when I thought, 'I want to be on TV.'" Did she stop to consider what a big challenge that could be? Not at all! "It looked easy," she confessed, "and fun, and I think every kid wants to be on TV."

A lot of kids, if they did seriously consider being on TV, would simply announce they wanted to do it and leave it at that, waiting for the world to somehow make it happen. Not Victoria, though! "I was watching this Pringles commercial and I thought, 'I could do that, and how can I start doing that?'" she told *Justine* magazine. She already knew exactly where to go when she needed help—her mom! "I don't think I ever said to my mom, 'I want to act!'" she was quick to explain to *Scholastic*. "I just liked being funny and entertaining people. I was always putting on shows with my friends and my sister." But even if Victoria never put it in precisely those words, she wasn't shy about making her wishes known. "After I told my mom I wanted to [act]," Victoria continued, "she found an agent in South Beach."

Why South Beach? That's a good question! It's not like Hollywood is a tiny town—with over five million residents, it's the twelfth largest city in the state of Florida! Miami is the largest urban area in Florida, however, and has far better connections for acting and modeling. And South Beach, which is a twenty-three-block stretch of Miami Beach (a part of the larger Miami area), is one of the world's top locations for fashion shoots. Its prominence makes Miami the model shoot capital of the United States. That's why Victoria's mom thought to look there for an agent. She knew finding representation in South Beach would give her little girl a lot more opportunity.

And it worked! Victoria found an agent, who quickly got her an audition for a commercial. It was for a national ad campaign, too—talk about starting off big! And Victoria nailed the audition, and won the part!

"My very first commercial was for Ovaltine," she recounted to justjaredjr.buzznet.com, "and I was so excited when I got that job. I was on the verge of tears when they called me and said that I got it. I even remember my three lines perfectly! 'It's choclatey! Ovaltine's amazing! More Ovaltine, please!' I felt like a star after I did that, even though the conditions [on set] were terrible—there was no trailer and it was really cold. I was just sitting outside with the rest of the kids huddling for warmth. But I couldn't have been happier—I was ecstatic!"

That was 2001 and the start of Victoria's career, but it was obvious to everyone that it wouldn't be the end. Far from it! She'd been bitten by the acting bug. She was determined to do more commercials, and then some!

CHAPTER 3
FROM HOLLYWOOD TO HOLLYWOOD

Victoria's agent kept finding her auditions, and she kept landing the jobs. "I think I've done about thirty commercials," she told justjaredjr.buzznet.com. She was rapidly becoming an in-demand child star, and not just for commercials. Victoria's unique look also meant that she could book a lot of jobs as a child model, and she did. She quickly found herself busy with both television commercials and photo shoots that required her to model.

And South Beach was a great place to be, especially for a young girl getting into modeling. "South Beach is absolutely beautiful, and so much fun!" Victoria told *Scholastic*. "There are so many great restaurants, cool boutiques, and beautiful hotels. I have great memories of modeling on the beach, and then when I was done, my mom and I would go have dinner somewhere. It was great!"

But was that enough for Victoria? Not by a long shot! Photo shoots were fun but you didn't get to do anything except pose. Commercials were better but still really limiting—you weren't even playing a character. You were just showing off a product. Victoria wanted to work on a project she could really sink her teeth into. She wanted to act! "It's great to get a script of a character and make it come alive," she told the *Hollywood Reporter.* Even before she'd tried it herself, she already had a sense of how it would be—". . . one day I just realized that the thing that I wanted to do and that my dream in life was to act," she confided to *Starry Constellation* magazine. No doubts in Victoria's mind. This was a girl with a goal.

But there weren't a lot of acting jobs available in Miami, and especially not for a child star. If Victoria really wanted to act, she'd have to head to the other Hollywood—the famous one. Hollywood, California: Home of the television and movie industries.

"I told my mom that I really wanted to get into TV and movies because I really thought I could do it," she told justjaredjr.buzznet.com. Fortunately, Serene (Justice) Reed believed in her daughter, and in her talent! "She agreed," Victoria explained, "and when I was 11, we packed up and moved to Los Angeles! We just packed our suitcases—me, my mom, and my sister . . . my step-dad had to go back and forth between Florida and California because he had to work."

It was a big move for such a little girl, especially since Victoria hadn't booked any acting jobs in California yet. After all, what if they got all the way to Los Angeles and Victoria couldn't land any roles? Serene believed in her daughter's talent, but it was still a huge risk to take. Fortunately, the Reeds were a pretty practical family. They were happy to support Victoria's pursuit of her dreams, but they also wanted to keep the family safe and secure. So how did they balance those two factors? "Well, we only came for the summer," Victoria admitted to justjaredjr.buzznet.com, "because I wasn't really expecting anything."

Even at eleven, Victoria was already too smart and too sensible to assume she'd make it big right away. She understood that this way, they had a few months to give it a shot and to see how they liked California—and how it liked Victoria! But they still had their home in Florida, and their friends back there, and the girls had school waiting for them in the fall. It was a smart move, and one that would ultimately pay off big. It also explains why Victoria is still so grounded, even today when she's getting starring movie roles left and right. She began her career sensibly, and that really paid off for her in the long run.

CHAPTER 4

ONE OF THE GIRLS

It was the summer of 2003. Victoria and her family had just arrived in Hollywood, California. She was eleven years old. Her parents immediately began looking for an agent for her, and quickly found one. They settled on a man named Mitchell Gossett, who worked for Cunningham, Escott & Dipene, or CED, one of the top talent agencies in Los Angeles. CED, which later became Cunningham, Escott, Slevin & Doherty, or CESD, boasted an extremely strong Young Talent division—Mitchell also handles such young celebrities as *Hannah Montana* star Miley Cyrus; AnnaSophia Robb, who is best known for her role as Violet Beauregarde in 2005's *Charlie and the Chocolate Factory*; *Heroes* star Hayden Panettiere; singer Jesse McCartney; Kristen Bell, who voices the character of Gossip Girl on the hit CW series of the same name; and many others. He clearly has a good eye for talent: He signed Victoria immediately! Then he got to work finding her acting jobs.

It didn't take him long, despite the fact that Victoria didn't have any previous acting experience, just various roles in commercials. Within three weeks of their arriving in California, Victoria had her first television role! And it was on one of the WB's biggest hits: *Gilmore Girls*! *Gilmore Girls* is a Golden Globe-nominated, comedy-drama series starring Lauren Graham and Alexis Bledel as a mother-daughter duo. It aired for seven seasons, from 2000 through 2007, on the WB and later the CW network. It was even named one of the top 100 television series of all time by *Time* magazine! Needless to say, Victoria was thrilled to be joining the cast for an episode.

The episode Victoria guest starred on was the Halloween episode, entitled "The Hobbit, the Sofa, and Digger Stiles." It took place in the fourth season of the show, and aired on October 7, 2003. In this sixty-eighth episode of the hit series, Lorelai, played by Lauren Graham, and Sookie, played by Melissa McCarthy, decide to make some extra money to pay for their new inn by becoming caterers. Their first gig winds up being a *Lord of the Rings*-themed children's party. This was where Victoria came in. She played a hobbit! "I had one line," she later told the *Hollywood Reporter*. "I was dressed in a heavy robe, and it was 103 degrees." Did she mind? Not at all! "I didn't care," she recalled. "I was so thrilled to be on a set!"

Pleased at how quickly that first job had emerged, Victoria's parents debated what to do next and finally decided to extend their summer vacation an extra month. They told Victoria's agent, and he quickly started scouting more projects for her. What he came up with was something a little different. For one thing, it was a thriller. For another, it wasn't television! Victoria Justice was about to hit the big screen!

Victoria was thrilled when she heard she had an audition for a part in a movie. She'd loved being on a television set, and definitely wanted to do more there, but she was also excited to see if she could act in films. Plus, working in a movie meant that she could add yet another talent to her growing résumé.

Victoria's first film audition was for an

independent film called *Fallacy*. Even though the film had a small budget and was only slated for a limited release, it still boasted a powerful cast, including John Savage (who voiced the role of Beast in *Beauty and the Beast*), Gary Busey (nominated for an Oscar for his performance as Buddy Holly in *The Buddy Holly Story*), and Stephen Baldwin (one of the famous Baldwin brothers, who has starred in a lot of popular movies like *Bio-Dome* and *Fred Claus*). Veteran stuntman Jeff Jensen had decided to try his hand at directing a few years before, with a movie called *High Speed*, and *Fallacy* was his second directorial effort. He had also written the script, based on a story by Mark Daniel Jones. Jensen liked Victoria, and decided to cast her in a supporting role.

Fallacy is a mystery-thriller about a deceptive society where you can't buy freedom, but you can steal it. Victoria had a great time working on the movie, and being around actors with such amazing work histories was a real education for her. She decided she definitely liked performing on both the big and small screens, and eagerly went after auditions in both venues.

Victoria's roles on *Gilmore Girls* and *Fallacy* were her first real taste of acting, and she loved it! This was probably when she decided that this was what she wanted to do with her life. But acting jobs were tough to come by, especially for someone with such limited experience, and the summer ended without her landing another acting gig. This meant it was time to return home. The family headed back to Florida, where Victoria and her sister returned to school. By the time the *Gilmore Girls* episode aired on October 7, she was already back in her normal routine.

But that didn't mean Victoria had forgotten what it had been like to be on a set. Not at all! She knew education was important and she was glad to be home and with all her friends again, but she'd enjoyed her experience far too much to quit acting. She knew when summer rolled around again, she and her family would be heading back to California. And this time, Victoria was determined to get more than one line!

CHAPTER 5
THE HEIGHT OF FASHION

For the rest of 2004, Victoria concentrated on two major things: her schoolwork and planning her return to California the next summer. But while she wasn't busy studying or dreaming of all the acting roles she'd land the next time her family went out to California, she was busy with something else: making a name for herself in the world of modeling. Luckily for Victoria, modeling was something she could do while living in Florida—she didn't need to be in California to get all the really big gigs.

And, as with everything she did, Victoria didn't just dabble in modeling, playing background in a few small shoots while she planned her big acting breakthrough. No, Victoria threw herself into her modeling career with all her typical enthusiasm and energy. And, as it often did, her 100 percent commitment paid off. Big-time.

In the modeling world, there are onetime photo shoots and there are ad campaigns. Every model wants to land an ad campaign—it's exactly like the difference between a guest star spot on a television show and being cast as a regular on a series. Ad campaigns are ongoing, with a series of photo shoots, magazine spreads, commercials, and billboards. They're usually for major companies with famous brands, and involve a great deal of money. It's good, steady work for the model, and pays top dollar. Plus, it's amazing exposure. A lot of really famous actresses started out as models, like *Charlie's Angels* star Cameron Diaz, who was signed to Elite Model Management when she was only sixteen years old! Knowing this was probably great inspiration for Victoria.

Not surprisingly, companies with kid-related products produce kid-friendly ads, typically using child models. A bunch of really big companies have kid-based ad campaigns. And three of the biggest are Gap, GUESS, and Ralph Lauren.

Gap began as a single store on Ocean Avenue in San Francisco, California, opened by Doris and Don

Fisher in 1969. According to Don Fisher on their website, "I created Gap with a simple idea: to make it easier to find a pair of jeans." Over the years, Gap grew into a major clothing brand, best known for its jeans but also for its casual, comfortable, trendy clothes. Gap, Inc. eventually expanded to include three other brands: Banana Republic, Old Navy, and Piperlime. They distinguish the brands by saying that Gap is "iconic American style," Banana Republic is "accessible luxury," Old Navy is "great fashion at great prices," and Piperlime is "the insider's guide to the best shoe and handbag brands."

GUESS also started as a jeans company in California, though it began a few years after Gap, in 1981. Its founders, Maurice and Paul Marciano, came from southern France and wanted to infuse American blue jeans with style and class. Retailers weren't sure these strange, new jeans would actually sell, and Bloomingdale's only agreed to carry two dozen pairs as a personal favor to the brothers. But when they sold out within hours, the store knew they had a hit, and a new direction for fashion denim was born. Now GUESS is world-famous and world-renowned, and produces everything from shoes to watches to eyewear to jewelry, selling these products all over the world.

American designer Ralph Lauren established the Polo label in 1967 with a line of ties. The wide, handmade, flamboyant ties quickly became a status symbol. By 1969 he had a store within Bloomingdale's, and in 1971 he launched both his first women's clothing collection and his first store in Beverly Hills, California. Ten years later, Ralph Lauren opened its first international store in London. During the 1980s, the polo shirt, a short-sleeved, knit shirt with the polo player logo on the left breast, became the indispensable clothing choice of the preppy set. Ralph Lauren has since expanded his lines to include all men's and women's clothing, plus luggage, leather goods, and jewelry. In 2003, Ralph Lauren became the official clothing outfitter for Wimbledon, the world's premiere tennis competition. In 2005, Polo became the official apparel sponsor for the US Open, America's major tennis competition. And in 2008, Ralph Lauren won the contract to outfit the 2008 US Olympic team.

Three of the biggest, best known, and most important adult *and* kids' clothing companies in the world. Three of the largest kids' ad campaigns. And Victoria Justice? She landed all three of them in 2004!

It was unbelievable. Any model would consider herself incredibly lucky to book even one of those campaigns. To get all three at once? It was instant, worldwide fame! One of the most memorable images was a full-spread GUESS ad featuring Victoria and two other girls, their heads together as if sharing a secret. The photo is outdoors, a suggestion of a beach or desert somewhere behind them. The girls are dressed warmly and are each wearing hats—on the right, Victoria wears a tan knit sweater and a matching knit cap, her bangs just dusting her brow, her long, straight hair framing her face and warm smile. At the time, the image was really popular, and it appeared everywhere! Victoria Justice was now one of the most celebrated child models in the world.

Many models might decide that this was the top of their career, the absolute pinnacle, and walk away afterward. After all, how could you top working for Gap, GUESS, and Ralph Lauren in a single year? Others would accept that they were now modeling superstars and would go on to focus entirely on modeling, becoming major supermodels and getting similar ad campaigns, but for adult clothing lines and products. What did Victoria do? Always one to follow her own heart and trust her own instincts, she did neither!

Victoria continued to work in modeling, but never as intensively as she did in 2004. She knew that year might be the height of her modeling career, but rather than worry about not having as much success later, she chose to enjoy it while it lasted, and then focus on other things. She didn't try to turn her child modeling success into an adult supermodel role, because she already had her heart set on other roles. Acting roles.

Victoria was still intent upon being an actor. She'd already had a taste of acting in both movies and television. Now she was ready for more. She hoped that her recent success in modeling would make her more appealing to casting directors, since she was now a recognizable face, and that this would offset her lack of experience. But whether it did or not, she was determined to continue auditioning for roles until she got her big break. Modeling was fun and rewarding, and she was glad she'd done it and would continue to model occasionally after 2004. But for Victoria, her big break as a model was just a stepping stone on the way to similar successes in the acting world.

CHAPTER 6

BACK TO L.A.

In the summer of 2004, Victoria and her family returned to California. During the year, while Victoria and her family were living in Florida, Victoria's agent in L.A. had been hard at work, looking for promising auditions for the up-and-coming star. Victoria was thrilled to learn that he had found several auditions for her while she was gone. It was great to get back to California and already have things lined up, even if none of those jobs were a sure thing. Still, things were definitely moving faster than they had in 2003, and that was a good sign.

Victoria's next role was on film, and it was a bigger part than she'd had in *Fallacy*. This time she was cast in *When Do We Eat?*, a quirky film about a Passover Seder (the formal dinner held on the first two nights of the Jewish holiday) gone horribly,

Party of Five, *Wings*, and *Married with Children*, played the Shrink. Suzie Pollard of *Foxworthy's Big Night Out* and *Beyond the Break* played the Virgin Mary.

Playing the lead, even in such a tiny movie, was a completely new experience for Victoria—and she adored it! Some of that may have been the fact that it was an independent short film, however, so it was free of many of the complications you might encounter in a big-budget movie. "The crew were some of the nicest people I've ever worked with," Victoria wrote on her official website, victoriajustice. net. "Aaron [Ruell] is such a wonderful director, and a very kind person. I would love to work with him again. His wife Julia, who is so nice as well, appeared in the film, and also did the editing."

Mary was filmed in the beginning of August, which was cutting it a bit close for Victoria—she and her family still had to make it back to Florida in time for the new school year! Taking the lead was definitely an opportunity she couldn't pass up, however. And it proved to be a wise choice when *Mary* went on to become a 2005 Official Sundance Film Festival Selection. The Sundance Film Festival is one of the most prestigious film festivals in the world, and to win recognition there has made many an actor, director, and writer's career. Victoria and her parents certainly hoped the accolade would work its magic for her!

Once again, Victoria had a great time working on set. And in both movies, she got to work with wonderful casts, all of them far more experienced than she was, and therefore, able to teach her a lot. That summer was a real opportunity for Victoria to learn more about the craft, and about the business of making movies. Unfortunately, the summer soon ended, and it was back to Florida for Victoria and her family. But her first starring film role had made it abundantly clear to everyone that the eleven-year-old had a definite future in Hollywood, and not the one on the east coast. On their way back to Florida, after filming on *Mary* wrapped, Victoria and her family were already planning their return trip next summer!

CHAPTER 7
SCHOOL AUDITION

Victoria and her family had now spent two years shuttling back and forth between Hollywood, Florida, and Hollywood, California. They were happy they'd done it, since Victoria had found great success both times, but uprooting for the entire summer was a stressful process, and took a lot out of all of them. It was clear they couldn't keep moving back and forth year after year. Something would have to change.

It was also clear that, while Victoria had tremendous natural talent, she still had a lot to learn. The finest natural actor can benefit from proper training. And if she wanted to take real acting classes, Florida just wasn't going to cut it.

Fortunately, Los Angeles (specifically, Sherman Oaks) was home to the world-renowned Millikan Middle School and Performing Arts Magnet.

Victoria auditioned for the performing arts school during the summer of 2005. The admissions board contacted her family a short while later—Victoria had been accepted into their musical theater program!

It was perfect. Now that Victoria's education was squared away, the family could move to Los Angeles for good, and stay there year-round. Victoria's stepfather, Mark Reed, could find a new job there and not have to worry about taking time off from work each summer to travel across the country. Victoria's sister Madison could settle in and make new friends that she wouldn't have to leave behind each fall. And so could Victoria.

This also meant that Victoria could take acting jobs during the year instead of only during the summer. Her agent was thrilled—Victoria was becoming a hot commodity, and only being able to accept jobs that filmed in the summer had severely limited her options. Now her agent could find her auditions year-round, and she wouldn't have to leave home to take them. In fact, if they worked things out carefully, she might not even need to miss school!

Of course, Victoria's family could have avoided the school problem altogether if they had simply decided to homeschool her. "Most kids that are in the entertainment business are home-schooled," Victoria told *Supermodels Unlimited* magazine. It made sense, really—that way the parents and tutors could make sure the kids got a proper education, but could tailor their study and classroom hours to fit the shooting schedule of whatever show they were currently doing.

There were drawbacks to homeschooling, however. You didn't have the same interaction, for one thing—you never had classes with other kids, so you didn't encounter as many different people your own age. It also made it much harder to make friends, particularly non-industry friends. Homeschooling also meant a more flexible course schedule, which wasn't always a good thing. "We try to keep everything really grounded," Victoria's mother explained to *Quince Años* magazine. "With money and fame it's very easy for things to get out of hand. The kids [on the film set] are very catered to and get accustomed to it, with this sense of entitlement. But that is not reality with the rest of the world, it's not the way it really works."

That's why Victoria continued to go to a real school instead of being homeschooled. "My mom and I decided that I would go to a public school so that my life wouldn't change very much," she explained to *Supermodels Unlimited* magazine. "We decided I would go as long as I possibly could, until I couldn't do it anymore."

It wasn't always easy. Even at the Performing Arts Magnet, Victoria was a rarity—most of the kids there wanted to be in entertainment someday, but few of them already were. And Victoria was getting more and more work all the time! After the move to L.A., she landed two more national commercials, one for the department store chain Mervyn's and one for Peanut Butter Toast Crunch cereal, and a regional commercial for the Los Angeles Dodgers. She tried her hand at theater, performing in productions of *Annie*, *Give My Regards to Broadway*, and *Tribute to Disney*. She went out for various film and television roles. Other kids at school began to recognize her, and not just because they passed her in the halls.

"I learned to tell the difference on who wanted to be my friend because they really liked me or who just wanted to be friends with the girl who was on TV," Victoria admitted to *Supermodels Unlimited* magazine. "I absolutely became more guarded on who I associated with. There would be times I would be sitting in a classroom, or walking down a hallway and someone would whip out a cell phone and take a picture of me, which was weird."

Victoria persevered, though. Education was important to her, and to her family. So was having as close to a normal life as possible. Fortunately, not everyone acted differently around her. "All my friends treat me the same," she told teenhollywood.com. That was one of the nice things about attending a regular school— that she had friends who weren't actually in the entertainment industry. But she was also starting to make friends with other actors, and that was good as well because they understood what it was like to have early-morning calls, late-night revisions, and crazy rush shooting schedules.

It was a difficult life, but Victoria managed it gracefully and with a smile, just as she managed everything else. Besides, she was in Los Angeles, with her family around her, doing what she wanted to do. What could be better?

CHAPTER 8
THE SUITE LIFE

One of 2005's hottest shows was *The Suite Life of Zack & Cody*, which premiered on the Disney Channel on March 18, 2005. Created by Danny Kallis and Jim Geoghan, the sitcom starred Dylan and Cole Sprouse as a pair of trouble-making twins, Zack and Cody Martin. On the show, the twins live in the Tipton Hotel in Boston, because their mother Carey sings and performs in the hotel lounge. The twins frequently get themselves in trouble, often with the aid of the hotel owner's ditzy daughter London and the down-to-earth candy counter girl Maddie, and frequently butt heads and match wits with Mr. Moseby, the strict hotel manager. The Sprouse brothers had become instant teen heartthrobs and the show landed huge ratings and an enormous overnight fan base. A role on this show was the hottest ticket in town. So what did Victoria do? She landed herself a guest starring role!

Victoria played the part of Rebecca on the episode "The Fairest of Them All," which aired on March 18, 2005. It was only the second episode of the show ever to air! Of course, the episode had actually been shot much earlier than that. "I filmed *The Suite Life of Zack and Cody* in September 2004, for an entire week," Victoria said on her website.

September 2004? Wouldn't that mean it was right after *Mary*, and before she and her family headed back to Florida for the start of the 2004-2005 school year?

Absolutely. "That was actually one of my very first things that I did on TV," Victoria told thestarscoop.com. "And it was in front of a live audience so that was extremely cool." A live audience can be intimidating, even to a natural-born performer like Victoria! "At first I was really nervous," she admitted to thestarscoop.com, "because that was the first time I had ever done anything like that. Everyone was really nice on set, and they made me feel really warm and welcome. Fun."

The episode centers on a Mini Miss beauty

pageant. Zack and Cody want to buy new bikes but can't afford them. Then the beauty pageant comes to the Tipton and somehow Cody accidentally winds up entered in it. He develops a crush on one of the contestants, Victoria's character Rebecca, and he agrees to stay in the contest just so he can spend time with her. Zack, meanwhile, sees Cody's participation as a chance to win the prize money and buy those new bikes, after all. When Cody states that he likes Rebecca too much to get in the way of her winning, he and Zack come to blows.

Victoria had a great time on the show. "The twins were so much fun," she wrote on her website, "and the rest of the cast were awesome. It was so much fun that I didn't want it to end! As a matter of fact, for a long time afterwards I would visit the set almost every week, when they would have their live studio audience performances on Tuesdays. Everyone always made me feel so welcomed, I will never forget this experience. I will always be very grateful to two amazing casting directors, Lisa London, Catherine Stroud, and the producers of this show for giving me this opportunity."

Of course, the show didn't premiere until the following March, so at the time no one knew what a huge hit it would become. "The Fairest of Them All" was the third episode they shot, but the network liked it so much, they decided to air it as one of the back-to-back episodes for the show's premiere. Needless to say, when the show came out and the fans went wild, Victoria's status skyrocketed— especially among teenage girls! All of them wanted to be where she'd been, with one (or both!) Sprouse brothers crushing on her. And with her kissing one of them! Rumors even circulated that she had dated one or the other of the twins, but Victoria denied them all, saying they were just friends. Even if the rumors weren't true, it was great publicity for Victoria. A guest spot on a hit TV show *and* a rumored romance with one of the hottest teen stars? Things were looking up for Victoria!

CHAPTER 9
NOT SO UNKNOWN

After *The Suite Life of Zack & Cody*, Victoria lucked into another amazing role—this time as a regular on a brand-new series! David Franzke, who had directed and produced episodes of both the *Jamie Kennedy Experiment* and the MTV hit *Punk'd*, was developing a series pilot for NBC. The show was called *Little Monsters*, and Victoria got cast as one of the regulars! Unfortunately, the show didn't get picked up and the pilot never aired—no one today even knows exactly what it was about! But it was still exciting for Victoria, and great experience as well. It showed her that she had the star power to book a regular job on a series. She knew it was only a matter of time before she had another shot at television stardom.

In the meantime, Victoria had plenty of work to do. In 2005 she had more luck. She got cast in a new movie, *The Garden*, and then in a made-for-television Christmas movie called *Silver Bells*. The year 2005 wound up being an extremely busy one for her!

Filming *The Garden* was a new experience for Victoria. She had done sitcoms and shorts and comedies, but this was her first horror movie! The story centers on a troubled, young boy named Sam (played by Adam Taylor Gordon, who also starred in *Cheaper by the Dozen* and *Cellular*) and his father (played by Brian Wimmer, who starred as Boonie on *China Beach* and Dr. Keith Ricks on the first season of *Flipper*). Sam had been in a mental hospital and, after his father David picks him up to bring him home, they get into a car accident. An old farmer named Ben Zachary (played by veteran actor Lance Henriksen, best known for the lead in the television series *Millennium* and for his role as the android Bishop in *Aliens*) finds them and nurses them back to health on his ranch. Then he offers David a job. David accepts, and enrolls Sam in the local school. But Sam is still having the same bad dreams that landed him in the hospital to begin with—dreams about an old, gnarled tree that just happens to exist on Ben's property! His schoolteacher is currently teaching the class about the Garden of Eden—and the Tree of Knowledge. What is really happening here? Who is Ben? And what does he have planned for them? Claudia Christian (Susan Ivanova on *Babylon 5*) and Sean Young (Rachael in *Blade Runner*) also star in this terrifying film. Victoria plays Holly, one of Sam's classmates.

As usual, Victoria enjoyed her work immensely. "I started filming River to Havilah (a.k.a. The Garden) in March, 2005," Victoria reported on her website. "My character's name was Holly, and I was so surprised to find out that the boy who played the lead in the film, Adam Taylor Gordon, went to my school. I had a great time filming this, and met so many wonderful people. Our director, Don Michael Paul, was such a nice guy, Stephen Cannell (our exec. prod.) was great, and our crew, many of whom I became very friendly with, and would work with again in the next couple of months. Adam is talented and really nice, we had a lot of fun on set."

Victoria's next role in 2005 was in a completely different movie. Different in genre, different in tone, different in setting—different in almost every way. *Silver Bells* focuses on a pair of lonely souls who discover a second chance at love. A widowed New Yorker named Catherine O'Mara (played by Anne Heche, who won Emmys for her role as Vicky on *Another World* and had since been on *Everwood*, *Ally McBeal*, and hit movies such as *Six Days Seven Nights* and *The Dead Will Tell*) meets and bonds with a young man named Danny Byrne (played by Michael Mitchell, who went on to star in *Invasion*, *Phil of the Future*, and *Thief*) who has run away from his father. She doesn't realize that his father, Christy (played by Tate Donovan from *Partners*, *Friends*, and *The O.C.*), is the same man who tries to sell her a Christmas tree every year. The following year Christy, himself a widower, comes to New York once again to sell his Christmas trees. He and Catherine cross paths again, only to discover the connection Danny has forged between them, and to discover each other as a result.

"First of all I have always loved the 'Hallmark Christmas' movies," Victoria admitted on her website. "This movie has such a wonderful story that

I think that you will all enjoy it. It stars Anne Heche, Tate Donovan, Michael Mitchell, and Courtney Jines. Even though I have a small supporting role (5 or 6 scenes) I was so glad to be a part of it. It was so much fun working on this project."

Part of the fun with any job is learning from it, and with *Silver Bells*, Victoria learned a lot more than acting! "I had to learn to ice skate a lot better than I already knew," she explained on her website. "I had a wonderful ice skating teacher named Mary, who taught me so much in about 6 lessons. After each lesson, I realized how much I loved ice skating. Mary said I had a natural talent for it—after my 3rd lesson I was able to do a jump and a spin. If I had more time this is something I would want to do a lot more of. I also became good friends with my co-star, Courtney Jines, we had so much fun skating together. It's funny that I had to get pretty good at it, and in the movie you see me skate for just a few seconds."

Of course, Victoria didn't slow down at all after *Silver Bells*. No, by April 2005, she had thrown herself right into her next role, which was her biggest one yet! And this was also a different movie for her, a psychological thriller called *Unknown*.

Unknown's beginning and premise are true to its title. Five men wake up in a warehouse. They don't know how they got there, or even where it is—there's no one else around, and the building is locked down tight. None of them can remember anything else, either, including who they are. But they gradually discover that there was a kidnapping plot, and things somehow went wrong. Some of the five are the victims—and some are the kidnappers. But who is who? The movie slowly reveals details, through flashbacks and other clues, as the characters try to piece together who they are and how to survive when so much of their situation is truly unknown. The movie stars James Caviezel (who previously played Jesus Christ in the controversial *The Passion of the Christ*), Greg Kinnear (who won an Academy Award for Best Supporting Actor for his role in *As Good as It Gets*), Joe Pantoliano (who won an Emmy for his role on the hit HBO series *The Sopranos*), Barry Pepper (who won several awards for his role as Roger Maris in *61**), Jeremy Sisto (formerly on

Six Feet Under and now Detective Cyrus Lupo on *Law & Order*) and Bridget Moynahan (from *Sex and the City* and *Six Degrees*). Victoria played Caviezel's daughter Erin, primarily in flashbacks.

"It was an amazing experience to work with such an amazing actor," Victoria wrote on her website about acting with James Caviezel. "He is so nice, and really funny. I only have a few scenes in the movie, but we had a really good time in between them just joking around, and singing. He also talked to me about some of his experiences he had filming the movie 'The Passion Of The Christ', it made me feel very privileged that he shared that with me." That was only after she'd warmed up to him, though! "I was kind of intimidated at first," she admitted to kidzworld.com, "(I mean after all, he played Jesus in *Passion of the Christ*), but he was so much fun that I had a great time. I was so impressed that after we were joking around, he could very quickly just start crying and become so serious in scene. I don't want to give anything away, but right after that scene, I felt that I had been in the presence of one of our greatest actors. He was amazing!"

As with every role, *Unknown* brought Victoria new challenges and fresh experiences. "It absolutely was," she told kidzworld.com when asked if being in a thriller had been challenging, especially compared to some of her sitcom work. "*Unknown* is a psychological thriller that has some really dramatic and intense scenes. They couldn't be more different."

Some things were the same, though. "For me the process really wasn't any different," she told kidzworld.com, "just the script. They tell you the night before what scenes you will be working on the next day. You study your lines and then work on what choices you will make on how to act in that scene. There are rehearsals and discussions of the scene just like on a TV show. *Unknown* was an independent film that had a deadline to be finished by, so it moved very fast, just like a TV show would."

Unknown didn't release until 2006. And by then, Victoria knew *exactly* how fast a TV show could move!

CHAPTER 10
ACTING 101

Actors are called upon to produce emotions on cue. But sometimes? Sometimes life makes it easy for them.

Take the Christmas movie *Silver Bells* Victoria made in 2005. She was part of the choir, and was supposed to be happy—it's Christmas, after all! Well, normally Victoria doesn't have any problem being cheerful; it seems to be her natural state. But this time she had a little extra help. "Here's another reason 'Silver Bells' will always be special to me," she reported on her website. "I was rehearsing the song for the choir scene when I received the phone call that I had booked the role of Lola on *Zoey 101*. So when you see that big smile on my face in the choir scene . . . you'll know why."

Zoey 101 was a Nickelodeon show that had premiered in early January 2005. It starred Jamie

Lynn Spears, younger sister of pop star sensation Britney Spears, as Zoey Brooks. In the first episode, Zoey and her younger brother Dustin arrive at their new boarding school, Pacific Coast Academy. The school had been all-boys, and Zoey is in the first group of girls admitted after it became coed. She is in room 101 in her dorm building, which is where the show gets its name. The series follows Zoey, Dustin (played by Paul Butcher), her roommate and best friend Nicole (actress Alexa Nikolas), their other roommate Dana (Kristin Herrera), and their friends Chase (Sean Flynn), Quinn (Erin Sanders), Logan (Matthew Underwood), and Michael (Christopher Massey). The show was an immediate success, and made Jamie Lynn Spears a star. For the second season, however, the producers decided to shake things up a bit. Dana and Nicole had fought constantly, and Zoey frequently had to mediate between them. The producers decided to remove Dana from the lineup and introduce a new roommate, one who would get along better with Zoey and Nicole. This meant they were casting. And a lot of girls were interested in the part, which was no surprise—*Zoey 101* was a hit TV show on one of the most popular networks for kids. When Victoria heard about the part, she knew she had to have it!

"Then *Zoey 101* came along and they were looking for a new character on the show," she told thestarscoop.com. "I auditioned for that and I got a callback, and I got a screen test a couple days later, I got the call that I had gotten Zoey 101. I was extremely happy; I was bouncing up and down and screaming. That was a really great moment." Not only a great moment—it was the big break that she had been waiting for!

Victoria Justice joined the cast of *Zoey 101* in the first episode of the second season. Dana has joined a European Exchange Program, so Zoey and Nicole get a new roommate, Lola Martinez. "Lola is just outrageous," Victoria explained to *Starry Constellation* magazine. "She's funky with a great sense of style and she's independent. She's just a great character. She definitely inspires me to make fashion statement. She doesn't care what anyone thinks and is a leader, not a follower."

Independent, stylish, and a lot of fun? Gee,

doesn't sound like playing Lola was much of a stretch, does it? "We are similar in the fact that we both go to school," Victoria told *Scholastic*, "and we both love to act." That's right, Lola's an actress, too! And one with some pretty lofty goals! "Lola is an aspiring actress who wants to win an Oscar by age 19," Victoria admitted. An Oscar by nineteen? Was Victoria channeling her own ambitions there? "I'd love to!" Victoria told teenhollywood.com when they asked if she wanted to win an Oscar herself. But she's a bit more realistic than Lola. "My character's goal is to win one by 19 so I don't think that will happen for me but it would be awesome." You never know!

Of course, Victoria and Lola aren't exactly alike. Victoria's a bit more down-to-earth, and Lola is far more flamboyant, which made her great fun for Victoria. "I loved playing Lola because she was so glamorous," Victoria told *Supermodels Unlimited* magazine. "I was only twelve at the time when I landed the role of Lola, so for me it was a dream come true. I loved her clothes and her sense of style. There's always those few girls in high school that put a lot of effort in planning their outfits, makeup, hair and accessories. Lola was one of those girls and she made no excuses for it. She always looked great and had no problem speaking her mind. She said things others might want to say, but never would. I will always feel honored to have been cast to play her."

Does that mean Victoria doesn't dress up on her own? No, of course not. But she's a bit more selective about when and where. "I love clothes and dressing up as much as she does," she told *Scholastic*, "but not for school. I would never wear heels to school. I would wear either Converse or boots." Not Lola! For her, every day is an opportunity to look her snazziest! Of course, it helps that their school, PCA, is set up like a college campus, complete with rec rooms and lounges and restaurants. Victoria's real school was a little more traditional in appearance, which made dressing that fancy a little less likely.

Victoria spent the next three years on *Zoey 101*. It was a lot of work, of course. "It takes a week to film one episode," she told teenhollywood.com, "and usually we work from 7am until 8pm or sometime we only have to work for a couple of hours." But it was also a lot of fun. "I think the show is so amazing," Victoria gushed to *Starry Constellation* magazine. "The characters are wonderful and so are the directors and the executive producers. Everyone is just great! This is a great thing to get because there are kids on it my age. I'm so amazed that I even got the chance to do this."

Over the next three seasons, Victoria had a lot of great experiences. And some silly ones as well. "There is one time I can think of," she recounted to *Scholastic*, "which involves Matt Underwood [who plays Logan]. We all sit together at this round table in the cafeteria for lunch, and we laugh and talk about everything. A totally unsuspecting Matt started sipping his drink, and we all started laughing, because there was ranch dressing at the bottom of his glass. We all thought it was pretty funny, including Matt. As for who put it there, I'm not mentioning any names." Uh-oh! Could it have been Victoria herself? We may never know!

Not that Victoria didn't have her own share of embarrassments! And some of those were her own fault! "I had a flipper (a false tooth) that I wore almost all of the second season," she revealed to the *Hollywood Reporter.* "I was eating lunch, put it on my tray, forgot it was there and then threw it away. (When) we were called back to the set, I realized what happened. We frantically searched through the garbage but couldn't find it, so my dentist made an emergency dental visit to the set with a new one he just made." Whoops! Talk about an embarrassing moment!

Embarrassing moments aside, there were lots of great episodes over the years. Some actors hate to see themselves on-screen—it can make them uncomfortable and cause them to second-guess their acting choices. Not Victoria! "I love watching the episodes after they are done," she told teenhollywood.com. "When you're filming you don't really know how it's going to turn out after they add all the special effects and sounds and stuff."

Surprisingly, though, when asked what her favorite episode was, Victoria told kidzworld.com, "It would have to be the premiere episode of the second season when they introduce my character.

I first get to play a sort of Goth girl who has a real dark side, but as the show goes on, you find out I'm really an actress who is just having fun in an acting experiment. It was a blast! I loved my wardrobe and I loved the way they introduced my character. The best part of that episode was when I had to improvise this voodoo chant. It was so funny because I was making all these weird sounds and none of us could keep a straight face!"

Victoria obviously wasn't the only one who loved Lola. She was an instant hit with the viewers—and with the critics! In 2006, she, along with the rest of the *Zoey 101* cast, won the Young Artist Award for Best Young Ensemble Performance in a TV Series (Comedy or Drama). The show was also nominated for an Emmy Award for Outstanding Children's Program that year.

One of the advantages to being on a series is that you can build long-term relationships with the other cast, and with the crew. "*Zoey* is like going home," Victoria told kidzworld.com during one of the breaks between seasons, "because some of my closest friends are on that show. I know the crew

VICTORIA JUSTICE

VICTORIA shines on the red carpet at the 2008 MTV Video Music Awards.

VICTORIA and her *Spectacular!* costar Simon Curtis sign autographs for fans.

VICTORIA and actress Kirsten Prout dance the night away at the Teen Vogue Young Hollywood bash.

VICTORIA and her former *Zoey 101* castmate Jamie Lynn Spears reunite on the red carpet.

Hanging with fellow Nickelodeon stars Erin Sanders and Matthew Underwood at Nick's Slime Across America summer tour.

VICTORIA
with her buds
Simon Curtis
and Avan
Jogia at the
Hotel for Dogs
premiere.

Looking glam on
the red carpet at
the 2008 Kids'
Choice Awards
in a stylish
motorcycle jacket.

really well, all my castmates are awesome and we have so much fun together."

The cast members actually liked each other so much, they spent time together even when they didn't have to! "A lot of us live far from each other, so it makes it difficult to get together," Victoria once told *Scholastic*. "Jamie-Lynn goes back to Louisiana whenever she gets the chance, but I have spent a lot of time with Alexa, Matt, and Erin off set."

Putting a group of young actors together can sometimes be trouble. Victoria and her castmates would occasionally goof off onset, too, between takes. "Well, on the set there were these golf carts that we used to ride around in," Victoria admitted to justjaredjr.buzznet.com when asked about her favorite prop from the show. "We weren't allowed to drive ourselves around in the golf carts, but of course once we were told not to do that, we just HAD to get on them and drive around the set. We would sneak on those . . . that was a lot of fun."

Yes, clearly Victoria and Lola do have some things in common! Both of them love to have fun, and both of them like to do their own thing, especially if it means an adventure with friends! Like the time Victoria went bungee jumping: "I was with my friends at Six Flags," she told *Girl's Life*, "and I saw bungee jumping. I was like, 'It's going to be a memory we can share forever and tell our grandchildren.' As we were slowly going up, I started freaking out because you see everything getting smaller and smaller. But I would do it over and over again."

Of course, all good things must come to an end. After four seasons and four TV movies, the series finally ended with an hour-long finale called "Chasing Zoey." The final episode centered on the school prom, and on the main characters' relationships with each other. Lola had been dating Vince (played by Brando Eaton) for the end of the final season—Vince had been PCA's star football player until he had been kicked out for cheating (in the third-season episode "The Great Vince Blake") but he had returned a reformed man (in "Vince is Back" in season four)—and the two of them decide to show up to the prom fashionably late and almost miss it completely. The show ends with all of the main characters out on the dance floor, their various relationships finally resolved for the better: Zoey and Chase, Logan and Quinn, Lola and Vince, Michael and Lisa, and Mark and Stacey.

So how did Victoria feel after it was all said and done? "I didn't really think I would get so emotional, but I did," she confessed to *Supermodels Unlimited* magazine. "Actually, most of us did. I had spent three seasons on that series, and we had all grown up a lot, and gone through so many things together in those three seasons." It wasn't all crying, though. "I have amazing memories that I will always treasure and I'm really thankful that those years of my life are captured on film," she continued. "I'm not sad anymore because everything has to come to an end and we all have to move on. I'm very excited about the future."

Plus, just because the show ended doesn't mean the cast split up completely. "Erin Sanders is still one of my very best friends," Victoria told justjaredjr. buzznet.com. "I absolutely love her—she's crazy! Chris Massey, I'm still good friends with him. Matthew Underwood, I still talk to him occasionally, but he's been busy lately. Jamie Lynn, I haven't talked to recently. She's been going through some things, but she's a really nice girl, very down to earth, she's just like a normal Southern girl from Louisiana. I remember on the set, we would all freak out when she would bring fried okra to eat. We loved that, for some reason. She's really a normal girl, really sweet, and I wish her the best of luck in everything she does."

It shouldn't be any surprise that Victoria stayed friends with so many of her castmates. That's just the kind of outgoing, cheerful, friendly person she is. And she throws herself into each role so much, how could she not become emotionally attached both to her own character and to the others—and to the people who play them? "I have worked on a few projects, and I have to say that there was something I loved about all of them," she told kidzworld.com when asked to pick her favorite project so far. "If I had to choose though, it would be between *Zoey* and *Unknown*."

Certainly *Zoey 101* was a turning point for Victoria. Having that sort of stable, long-term job gave her the opportunity to be more choosy in her other acting roles, and to take more risks with them as well. It also let her develop a character over an extended period, growing Lola as Victoria herself grew. And since they were both preteens when they started, and were together for three long years, that's a lot of growth! In many ways Lola helped Victoria become the young adult she is today. "She's actually very cool," Victoria told *Scholastic* when asked about Lola. "You get the feeling that she's very confident and focused on her goal."

Yep, that definitely sounds familiar!

CHAPTER 11

LIFE AFTER LOLA

You would think, if you were cast as a regular in an ongoing—and wildly popular—television series, that you would spend all of your time and energy on that. Right? Well, not if you have energy to burn, like Victoria!

In addition to *Zoey 101*, her regular schoolwork, and hanging out with friends and family, Victoria was busy doing other projects.

The first of those was her guest spot on *Everwood*, another popular television show. *Everwood* ran on the WB for four seasons, from September 16, 2002, to June 5, 2006. It followed Dr. Andy Brown, a widower (played by well-known movie star Treat Williams), who leaves his neurosurgery practice in Manhattan and moves to Everwood, a small town in Colorado, with his teenage son Ephram (Gregory Smith) and his young daughter

Delia (Vivien Cardone). They choose Everwood because Andy's late wife had loved the place, and though it takes them a while to fit in, eventually the Browns come to love it there as well. Andy begins a tempestuous, on-again, off-again relationship with their next-door neighbor, Nina (Stephanie Niznik), while Ephram falls in love with the rival doctor's daughter Amy (Emily VanCamp).

Victoria guest starred on one of the last episodes of the series, "Enjoy the Ride," which aired on May 15, 2006. A young former medical student named Reid has just recovered from a failed suicide attempt and asks Amy out on a date. Amy agrees, despite still having feelings for Ephram, and talks her friend Hannah into a double date with Amy's friend Nick. Meanwhile, Delia is panicking because her Bat Mitzvah has fallen on the same day as Thalia Thompson's birthday party, and Thalia is the most popular girl in school. Nina is trying to resolve her feelings toward Andy and toward her former husband Jake, who has returned and asks her to move back to Los Angeles with him.

Victoria played the popular Thalia. It was an

exciting experience for her, especially since it was one of the few jobs she'd had that didn't take place in California! "They flew my mom and I to Utah," she reported on her website. "The weather was amazing. The other girls on set were great. 1 of them is Aree Davis, u remember her from the movie 'The Haunted Mansion', with Eddie Murphy. She also has a recurring role on 'Everybody Hates Chris', which is a new show on UPN. It's really funny, if u haven't seen it, u gotta tune in."

Naturally, Victoria made friends while she was out there. "Aree and I had a blast!!" she posted. "Vivien Cardone, who plays Delia on the show is so sweet. There was also another girl I met, Whitney Lee, she plays Britney on the show, she was really nice, too. We all had a great time!!! The roles might recur, so we might get 2 go back. It looks like our episode will air Dec. 8th, so ur gonna have to tune in."

In 2006, Victoria did something else she hadn't done before, at least not publicly—she sang! Singer-songwriter Vanessa Carlton had written a song called "A Thousand Miles" back in 2002, and had recorded it both as her first single and as part of her debut album, *Be Not Nobody*. The song was a breakthrough hit, and extremely popular throughout the year— it hit the top 5 in the United States, Ireland, and France, and the top 10 in the United Kingdom, Italy, and the Netherlands, and made it all the way to number 1 in Australia. The piano-driven pop song is about a young woman longing for her distant lover. *Billboard* magazine said, "It's the song's classical-tied piano hook that endures with urgency throughout the song that lends it spectacular charm, along with the artist's vulnerable vocal style." The song was nominated for three Grammy Awards—Record of the Year, Song of the Year, and Best Instrumental Arrangement Accompanying Vocalist—but lost out to Norah Jones's "Don't Know Why" for the first two and James Taylor's "Mean Old Man" for the last one. It did win Musicnotes' Song of the Year award in 2003, however. Billboard has since dubbed the song "one of the most enduring songs of the millennium." And Victoria recorded a cover of it!

Only—she didn't. At least, not deliberately. "There was a YouTube video where I covered 'A

Thousand Miles' by Vanessa Carlton," she admitted to justjaredjr.buzznet.com, "which I did just for fun with my singing coach. Somehow that got leaked online, and I guess people liked it." Which explains why the video is just a slideshow of images showing Victoria at various ages, in various shows and photo shoots, and with various friends and co-stars. Still, the video does show off her vocal talents—easy to see why people enjoyed it so much!

A few years later, however, Victoria did get to be in a music video. A real one. Only it wasn't hers!

"Hi everyone!" she wrote on her blog on April 24, 2008. "I'm going back to LA tomorrow to shoot a music video with a group called Menudo. Just in case u guys were wondering I don't do any singing or dancing in it, lol. I can't really release any info on the video, but I think it will be released really soon, (it's their 1st one). I've never filmed a music video before, but I think it'll be really cool, because it'll be different from anything I've done so far. I'll take pics to share with all of u." Of course, Victoria couldn't do just one thing! "I'm also shooting for a magazine cover that I'm really excited about on

Sat," she revealed. "I'll give more details when i fly back on Monday."

A few days later, she followed up about the video: "Hey everyone! I got back on Monday from shooting the 'Menudo' video, and I had a blast. The guys are all so nice and their music's really cool too, (check out their website-menudoworld.com). I brought my friend Audrey with me and we had a great time with the boys. They're all really down to earth and really sweet. They're really funny too. I can't wait for the video to come out . . . it's going to premiere really soon, (I think the end of this month). I'll keep u guys posted."

The video in question, "Lost," was released on June 24, 2008. The group is trying to stop a hostage situation, and Victoria plays the young woman they rescue. Unfortunately, the video, and the song, didn't get a lot of publicity, but it still received favorable reviews. It also introduced Victoria to the world of music videos and debut artists. Perhaps, given some of her recent musical activities, it even inspired her!

Meanwhile, Victoria was still involved with her first love as far as the entertainment industry goes: modeling! In April 2006, Victoria modeled again for the GUESS Campaign, and was excited to discover that one of her fellow models, Kelly, had been on the cover of the *American Girl* magazine issue that Victoria had recently been interviewed for. "She's really nice," Victoria confided on her website. "After we were done modeling we g2g riding on the go-karts together. I even came in 1st place once, it was so much fun."

A few months later Victoria had another modeling gig, this time for Union Bay's fall campaign. "Their clothes are really cute," she posted on her blog. Obviously she was still in demand as a model, and wisely chose not to ignore this aspect of her career. Modeling was fun for her, after all, and gave her an opportunity to meet new people and get still more exposure. Plus, she got to try on all kinds of cool clothes! What's not to love?

CHAPTER 12
SCHOOL . . . OF A SORT

Victoria did something else new in 2007—she switched schools! "I'm sorry I haven't been on in awhile," she posted on her website on September 19th of that year, "but it's been so crazy with starting a new school and everything, (I'm officially a freshman, yaay). I have to get up extra early just to go to this school, (like 5:45 a.m. everyday), to catch a school bus. It takes my bus about an hour to get there, but I have so much fun with my friends on it, (some old ones, and some new ones). It also gives me time to study for a test, and if I get hungry i just start eating my lunch, lol."

Victoria had been going to Millikan since her family had moved to Los Angeles two years before. Now, however, she became a freshman at Cleveland High School in Reseda, California. So how did she feel about the change? "I like H.S. a lot better than middle school," she admitted on her blog. "I guess because it's so much bigger, and I love so many of my classes. I'm in what they call the CORE program, which specializes in humanities/writing. I also love meeting so many new people. A lot of people don't recognize me, which is really cool because then I get to totally blend in." Leave it to Victoria to prefer that people don't know who she is! At least, not for her acting—we're sure, with her good nature and good looks, the other students discovered Victoria in a hurry!

Victoria didn't stay in high school very long, though. On June 14, 2008, she posted on her blog: "I just finished my 1st week at a junior college this week." Two weeks later, she'd already finished a college course of Spanish 1 (so yes, now she does speak at least a little Spanish!) and was starting geometry over the summer. Why over the summer? Because, as she posted, "I have to try to get ahead a little in school, because I have a lot coming up in the Fall."

Unfortunately, with Victoria's busy schedule, she wasn't able to keep up with regular high school *or* college courses the way she would have liked. That's why, on September 2, 2008, she wrote on her blog: "tomorrow's the 1st day of school, and for the 1st time ever I won't be having an official 1st day of school, because I'm home schooled now. I will be living vicariously through my sister Madison though, as my mom and I will be taking her tomorrow for her 1st day of 7th grade. I'll still be doing school, just at home and by myself. I am a little bummed about not having to plan my outfit for the 1st day, (I always looked forward to that, lol), but on the up side, I can eat whenever I want, and I can take lots of breaks, lol."

Small wonder, given all the acting jobs she's been doing, and modeling, and singing, and everything else! Victoria and her mother had always said she would stay in a regular school as long as it worked out, and she managed it far longer than most young stars with anything like her workload. Victoria also has a strong work ethic and had always gotten really good grades, so her parents didn't have to worry about her slacking off now that she was homeschooled. Plus, being homeschooled gave

Victoria more time to develop her career. And she'd really need it! Little did she know that her next big break was just around the corner.

CHAPTER 13
SPECTACULAR!

In April 2008, Victoria started work on a new project, her first major role since finishing *Zoey 101*. This was another project for Nickelodeon, but it was a little different than anything she'd done before. First of all, it was an original movie—and she had one of the starring roles! Second, and even more challenging for her—it was a musical!

The project was called *Spectacular!;* "It's a made for TV movie for Nickelodeon," Victoria reported to *Supermodels Unlimited* magazine. "It's a performance based movie and there's a lot of dancing and singing in it. It's kind of like *Bring It On*, but instead of cheerleading, it's a battle of the show choirs. I am so excited about this movie for so many reasons. One of them is because I make my singing debut. Nickelodeon is very excited about this movie too. It should air early 2009 also."

In the movie, Victoria plays Tammi Dyson, a snobby girl who's a lead singer in a show choir called Ta-Da. She and her boyfriend Royce Du Lac, played by Simon Curtis, have a bitter rivalry with Courtney Lane (Tammin Sursok), who leads the show choir called Spectacular! Things become even more heated when Courtney recruits a failed rock band singer, Nikko Alexander (played by Nolan Gerard Funk) to join her choir, and they start to give Ta-Da a run for their money. The national competition is coming up, and Tammi and Royce desperately want to win. So does Courtney, and she's convinced that Nikko's amazing voice can boost *Spectacular!* over the top, but Nikko still has his heart set on recording a rock album with his band and isn't sure he wants to be in a choir at all. His growing loyalty to the group—and his growing feelings for Courtney—start to change his mind, but will it be too little, too late?

Being in a musical was a lot of work, of course. "I've had to wake up at 8 in the morning and then dance for four hours straight and then I get a lunch break and then dance some more," Victoria reported to popstaronline.com, "but it's been so much fun! I could dance all day!"

As an added bonus, the movie was filmed in Vancouver, Canada. This meant that Victoria got to travel, which was always a fun experience for her. "It's an amazing city," Victoria posted on her blog in April. "The views are breathtaking. It has these incredible mountains that surround the Pacific Ocean."

Being her naturally outgoing self, Victoria also quickly bonded with the rest of the cast. "I've become really good friends with Simon Curtis, Andrea Lewis, (she plays Hazel on 'DeGrassi'), and Avan Joggia, (he has a movie coming out for Nickelodeon called 'The Gym Teacher' really soon)," she wrote on her website. The four of them spent a lot of time together, on-screen and off. "We were inseparable," Victoria reported to *Justine* magazine. "Like the Four Musketeers. We'd hang out, order room service, go shopping. It's funny because Simon lives five minutes away from me, so we see each other every day now."

While making the movie, Victoria and her

castmates didn't have a lot of time to goof off. That's because they were busy working! In addition to the regular acting, they had to learn the songs—and the dances! "We've had 2 weeks of intense dance rehearsals," Victoria revealed on her website, "and it's so much fun learning all the choreography. The rehearsals were everyday for 3 hours. I always wanted them to last longer, because I love dancing. We have a great cast, and they're all awesome!"

Of course, people were quick to compare the movie with other teen musicals, particularly Disney's popular *High School Musical*. "I think that people are comparing us to *High School Musical* because we do have music in *Spectacular!*," Victoria told Good Day LA, "but honestly, they weren't the first to do musicals. There were tons of musicals way before that."

Her co-star Simon Curtis added, "Triple threats are a big thing right now. You know—singing, dancing, acting. All three. We'd like to think we're capable of all three."

Victoria had proven plenty of times that she could act, and act well. And she'd shown on the leaked "A Thousand Miles" video that she could sing. But singing for a vocal coach and singing in a major television musical were two very different things! Was Victoria nervous?

She certainly didn't seem like it! "It was really fun," she told justjaredjr.buzznet.com about the recording process. "This is the first time that people are going to hear me sing officially . . . my voice will be on any soundtrack and people are actually going to hear me sing in the studio. It's really cool and I can't wait for people to hear it! The songs are really catchy and you can dance around to them. When we were filming, that's all me, Simon [Curtis], Avan [Jogia] and Andrea [Lewis], would listen to! We would dance around to the songs all the time and practice the moves."

Of course, it helped that Victoria was a quick learner. "I completed the songs pretty quickly," she told justjaredjr.buzznet.com. "I sang three songs that were all duets with Simon, and I finished them in 2 days. I practiced them a long time before, because I wanted to be prepared. So for the 2 weeks before that, I was rehearsing every single day, like 10 times a day. It's a good idea [to memorize the lyrics] because you're more prepared. I definitely did, but I don't think everyone does." Obviously those years of memorizing lines for *Zoey 101* and her other acting roles paid off here! As did Victoria's strong work ethic and attention to detail.

Filming for *Spectacular!* took close to a month because Nickelodeon wanted everything to be perfect. Victoria's favorite scene was the finale, "On the Wings of a Dream." "We all worked really really extra hard on that number," she told justjaredjr.buzznet.com. "Simon [Curtis] gets to lift me twice in that one, so that was really fun for me, even though I don't know if it was fun for him. He got close to dropping me a couple of times, but the main thing that kept happening was when the wings that were attached from my dress to my wrist would wrap around, and every time he tried to lift me up, it would get caught around his head! He would even start to choke! But it turned out pretty well."

Obviously Victoria had discovered a new love— for musicals! The show aired on February 16, 2009, on Nickelodeon, and performed well, capturing

3.7 million viewers despite being up against the Disney Channel's original movie *Dadnapped*. The DVD was released on March 31, 2009, but the soundtrack actually beat the movie out, releasing from Nick Records on February 3 and hitting number 44 on the Billboard 200 and number 1 on iTunes.

That's the recorded version, but justjaredjr.buzznet.com asked Victoria if she'd ever perform any of her songs live. "I would love to!" she replied. "I don't know if I'll ever get the opportunity to, but I think it would be so cool to do that at the Kid's Choice Awards or a morning show . . . I would love to do that!" Victoria had confidence in her musical abilities, and she wasn't the only one! She would soon find out that Nickelodeon was banking on her to become a music star. That's pretty *spectacular* news!

CHAPTER 14

A KING OR A QUEEN

Next up for Victoria was another movie, and this one had a theatrical release. Plus, it starred some of Victoria's old friends. "It's my 1st lead role in a feature film," she wrote on her blog on October 27, 2007, "and it's with 2 boys all of you know really well. I want you guys to guess who. I'll give you a hint, I've worked with them before when I was 11 years old."

The answer, of course, is the Sprouse twins, Cole and Dylan, whose show *The Suite Life of Zack & Cody* had been the site of Victoria's first major guest starring role. Now the three of them were reuniting for a film! "[It's] a family film called The *Kings of Appletown*," Victoria told *Supermodels Unlimited* magazine. "We had an amazing director, Bobby Moresco, who won an Academy Award for co-writing *Crash*. It's kind of a *Tom Sawyer* meets *Stand by*

Me. I play Betsy, whose father is accused of murder, and the twins and I set out to prove his innocence. It should be coming out in the beginning of 2009."

The film was shot down in New Braunfels, Texas, and Victoria had a great time offset exploring the area with the Sprouse brothers. There was an amazing steakhouse down there, she told justjaredjr.buzznet.com, and she went there all the time for their lamb chops and baked potatoes. "And we went paintballing! It was my first time! I wasn't afraid at all but of course my mom bought me a bright blue vest. I didn't know I was supposed to be camouflaged, so I looked like a little blueberry running around that field! I'm in this green forest, and I'm just this blue thing scurrying around! Everyone could see me and just get me every time! It definitely stung a lot. After a while, I had a couple of bruises. But I played hard! Just because it was a bunch of guys and me, I was determined. There was also an amazing hot tub, so we were in that a lot . . . we went go-karting . . . I did a lot of guy activities. I felt like one of the guys when I was there!"

Victoria did convince the boys to do things her

way from time to time, too. "It was soooo much fun to film!" she told kids.aol.com. "The twins are so much fun, I swear I was laughing like every second of filming. We were constantly singing and acting really stupid, which is always fun."

In the movie, Cole and Dylan play Clayton and Will, a pair of brothers who witness a murder. The police think they've found the culprit, but the twins know it wasn't him. Meanwhile, the man's daughter, Betsy, is devastated. "My character goes through a lot at the beginning of the movie," she told justjaredjr. buzznet.com. "She's really upset, everyone in the town has totally turned against her family, and she's just going through a lot of drama. Then I find out that the Sprouse twins know what really happened, so we go on this journey and adventure to prove that my dad is innocent."

The movie is rated PG for mild violence, mild language, and some crude humor. It had a limited preview release on December 12, 2008, before going back into post-production. The official release date has not yet been announced, but will be some time in 2009.

The Kings of Appletown was an exciting project for Victoria. Not only did she get to reunite with the Sprouse brothers, and do a feature film again, but she got to play one of the leading parts! It was certainly a major step for her and, once the movie releases, her name and face will be even more known across the country. This will no doubt be just the first of many leading film roles for the lovely Miss Justice!

CHAPTER 15
PLAYING ALONG

Victoria has a good nature, a good attitude—and a good heart. And she's been showing her heart for years by participating in a variety of charity events and community activities.

Back in April 2006, for example, Victoria, with her *Zoey 101* castmates Matt Underwood and Erin Sanders, took part in an event called Storytellers. "It's a special program where 10 elementary school children are chosen who have a special talent for writing," Victoria wrote in her blog. "They are then given mentors that are successful working actors in the business, who help them write a 4-5 page screenplay. Then, (this is where we come in), they ask working actors to come in, and perform their screenplays. So Matt, Erin, and I are performing this evening. It sounds very cool, because u don't get to rehearse, u just go with it."

The following month, she took part in a different program, the Celebration for the Arts. This was held on the Santa Monica Pier, and showcased Santa Monica and Malibu public school students in order to promote arts education. As stated on the 2006 flyer, "This year, many young celebrities will join in to let everyone know the importance of arts education in public schools. Their involvement sends the message that everyone should have the opportunity to be exposed to the arts! All of the activities will take place on the Santa Monica Pier and are a perfect choice for family fun!" Victoria was one of the young celebrities mentioned. She showed up with her friend Sarah, had fun, did a few interviews, and helped encourage everyone to have a good time and participate, so they could see just how important arts education really is, for both the students and the community.

A few weeks later Victoria had another project, this one both a paying job and a community service. She taped a commercial for Proposition 82, which ran near the end of the month. Proposition 82, launched by actor-director Rob Reiner on March

25, 2005, had been designed to create a universal preschool for all California children. Under the plan, all California four-year-olds would be offered a full year of preschool. In order to pay for the program, however, high-income taxpayers would have been hit with an additional tax. Apparently that was too much to ask, and when the proposition came up for a vote on the June 6, 2006, ballot, it lost 60.9 percent to 39.1 percent. Despite that, Victoria was glad that she had the opportunity to contribute to this cause.

On June 4, 2006, Victoria and her family went to a fundraising picnic for the Blind Baby Fund. As she described on her blog, "It's a fund raiser to try help pay for cornea transplants, and surgeries to help prevent blindness in babies. It was a meet & greet, along with a photo op with some other celeb teens, that I know you'll recognize. My sister, and my mom went also and we all had a great time."

Later that year, at the end of September, she and Matt and Erin, her *Zoey 101* castmates, and a bunch of others were back out on the Santa Monica pier. This time they were there to help raise money for a UCLA hospital. "We all took turns signing autographs," she said on her website, "and then we went on all kinds of rides that were there. We had an awesome time!!"

Of course, not every event Victoria did was designed to raise money. Some were just to raise enthusiasm—in her fans! One of the most exciting of those was in March 2008, when Victoria took part in the Xbox LIVE Game with Fame program.

Xbox is the bestselling video game console from Microsoft, which competed with Sony's PlayStation 2 and the Nintendo GameCube when it launched. Xbox was later replaced by Xbox 360, but one of the original console's best features was the Xbox LIVE service that allowed players to compete against each other in real time online.

The Xbox LIVE Game with Fame program was created to give Xbox LIVE subscribers a unique opportunity to meet, chat with, and play against some of today's hottest stars. Game with Fame celebrity players have included Shia Labeouf, Andy Roddick, Jack Black, Jenny McCarthy, Ludacris, Rihanna, and Ryan Cabrera. And on March 28, 2008, Xbox LIVE players had the opportunity to compete with two of Nickelodeon's hottest young actresses: Victoria Justice and Aria Wallace. Aria was the star of the Roxy Hunter television movies. She had also been on episodes of *The Bernie Mac Show*, *Charmed*, *Carnivale*, *CSI: NY*, *iCarly*, and others. She and Victoria were both attending the Nickelodeon Kids' Choice Awards, hosted by Jack Black, the next day, and had agreed to participate in the Game with Fame program first. Xbox LIVE players could sign up to play against Aria on *Dance Dance Revolution Universe 2* or against Victoria on *Guitar Hero® III: Legends of Rock*.

Leave it to Xbox to make sure both actresses were sufficiently handicapped—after her hours of dance training for *Spectacular!*, Victoria probably would have been too much for any competitors on *Dance Dance Revolution Universe 2!* Instead she got *Guitar Hero® III: Legends of Rock*, which, according to Team Xbox's ad for the event, "offers the ultimate rock experience with new wireless guitars, freshly added content and features including a multiplayer action-inspired battle mode, grueling boss battles, a host of exclusive unlockable content and visually stunning rock venues. Expanded online multiplayer modes allow axe-shredders worldwide to compete head-to-head for true rock status as they riff through a star-studded soundtrack, including master tracks by legendary artists such as Aerosmith, Guns 'N' Roses, The Rolling Stones, Beastie Boys, Rage Against the Machine and Pearl Jam, as well as original songs by guitar icons Slash and Tom Morello."

The girls, of course, had a blast. "It's so much fun," Victoria told kids.aol.com, "because we're playing with kids around the world live, which is really awesome." Of course, that doesn't mean she was any good at it! When asked which game she was better at, Victoria told kids.aol.com, "Probably Guitar Hero. But honestly I'm not that great at either one of them." Part of that, she admits, is because "I just started getting into video games actually, because I bought this big flat screen for my b-day and ps3. So now I've been playing rock band and guitar hero a lot. Rock Band's amazing too." Still, she had a great time, and the fans did, too—people signed on to play against her, or just to chat with her, and she and Aria had a good time hanging out as well.

Then in June 2008, Victoria went to New York City. "I had an awesome time," she wrote in her blog, "but it was a crazy schedule!! I had something going on practically every minute i was there. I had to do a lot of press, and a few photo shoots . . . I also did a lot of meet N greets." Despite that, she still found time to do another charity event—she and fellow *Spectacular!* star Simon Curtis attended a fundraiser for the Elizabeth Glaser Pediatric Aids foundation. Even when she's busy with other things, Victoria still finds time to make a difference. If you want to volunteer like Victoria, ask a parent to help you go online to find organizations in your area. If Victoria loves giving back to the community, you probably will, too!

CHAPTER 16
A BRIGHT FUTURE

So what exactly is Victoria doing now?

What isn't she!

For one thing, she's still modeling. She signed with Supermodels Unlimited not too long ago, and has already appeared in their magazine once for an interview and a photo spread. She's also modeling for La Senza Girl—Victoria and co-star Erin Sanders modeled for them once before, as part of La Senza's Fall 2006 fashion show to showcase the new *Zoey 101* collection, which was sold exclusively at La Senza Girl stores nationwide. Victoria and Matt Underwood had also done signings at several La Senza Girl stores in 2007 as part of the Family Channel's Spring Breakout Tour. La Senza Corporation is a Montreal-based company that provides exclusive fashion apparel for girls ages seven to fourteen—the stores are also designed to make tweens and their parents comfortable, as the company prides itself on its customer service.

Victoria's doing plenty of acting as well. She guest starred on two episodes of *iCarly* in early December 2008. *iCarly* premiered on Nickelodeon on September 8, 2007. The show stars Miranda Cosgrove as Carly, a thirteen-year-old girl from Seattle who creates her own web show, *iCarly*, with the help of her friends Sam (Jennette McCurdy) and Freddie (Nathan Kress). The series is all about Carly's life, and her efforts to maintain her web show, her schoolwork, and other normal teenage activities all at the same time. Sound familiar? Victoria probably felt right at home!

Unfortunately, while she was filming, Victoria came down with a nasty bug of some sort. On December 6, she wrote in her blog, "I'm working right now on a 2 parter on the I-Carly set, and I'm getting really sick. I guess a lot of the kids on this set are just getting over it, and it looks like I'm getting it. The role I'm playing is the most physically demanding role I've ever had to play. I'd tell you more, but I don't think I can without Nickelodeon's approval. But I will say I'm really sore and really bruised on my arms and a little on my legs."

Of course, even when she wasn't feeling well, Victoria still managed to have a good time. "The kids here are sooo nice," she reported. "Nathan is so sweet, and so are Jennette and Miranda. I've also met a couple of others that are awesome as well. Like the kid who plays Gibby, (Noah), and the kid who plays Nevils, (Reed). They're all really funny. Oh and I can't forget the incredibly funny Jerry Trainor . . . he's really so very nice. It's a great episode, that I can't wait for you guys to see. I don't know when it'll air, hopefully it'll be early 2009."

A month later, and fully recovered from her illness, Victoria was back in gear and ready to guest star on another hit teen show. "I started working as a guest star on *True Jackson, V.P.* today," she wrote on her blog on January 12, 2009. "Keke Palmer is such a sweet girl, and so is the rest of the cast." Victoria and Keke already knew each other a little bit from various Nickelodeon events and award shows. But this was the first time they had a chance to work together. Victoria already knew one of Keke's co-stars as well. "Robbie Ammel is in this episode, too," she wrote on her website. "You might remember him from *Picture This* with Ashely Tisdale. We've met a few times before at different events and he is also really nice."

True Jackson, VP premiered on Nickelodeon on November 8, 2008. Nickelodeon gave it a top spot, airing it right after the *iCarly* made-for-television movie: *iGo to Japan*. The first episode snagged an amazing 4.8 million viewers, and the show continued to perform extremely well and get excellent reviews. On December 15, only a month after it began, Nickelodeon approved *True Jackson, VP* for a second season. Clearly, they had a winner!

And now Victoria got a chance to guest star on the hit show! You would think she'd be completely relaxed about it—after all, she was on a hit Nickelodeon series herself for three years, and she'd been a guest star on other shows before! But there was one significant difference here. *True Jackson, VP* is filmed live!

Not that Victoria was worried! Well, not much, anyway. But she was excited, too. "Today we just did the table read and a rehearsal," she reported on her blog on January 12. "We will be taping on Thursday and Friday. I'm not sure when it will air, but I'll let you guys know when it does. And it's in front of a live studio audience which is sooo cool! The last time I did that was when I was 11 years old on the *Suite Life*." Ironic, then, that she'd be back in front of a live studio audience only a few months after her reunion with *The Suite Life's* stars, the Sprouse brothers!

On February 19, 2009, Victoria had another big moment. She turned sweet sixteen! Justjaredjr. buzznet.com had asked her a week before what she was planning to do to celebrate the occasion. Victoria's answer might surprise you! "It's weird," she told him, "because it's usually the kid that tells her mom that she wants a huge party, but my mom is the one trying to push me to have a party. I don't really know if I want one. I'm pretty much a low-key kind of person, not really glamorous or anything like that. It might be fun to have my friends come over and do that whole thing, but it's just so much work! I would just love to take my closest friends and go to Mammoth and go skiing and snowboarding. Because today, here in New York, is actually the first time I've ever been in snow! I've seen snow in pictures, and when I went to Utah, there was slush on the ground, but this is the first time I've been in falling snow!"

Then again, not wanting to make a big deal about herself isn't exactly out of character for Victoria. After all, this is the girl who went to public school and was thrilled at the thought that kids in her high school wouldn't recognize her from her television and movie work! She didn't do anything big for her previous birthday, either, and for most Latina girls the Quinceañera, or fifteenth birthday party, is a major event, welcoming the girl into adulthood. Families often throw elaborate Quinceañera parties and invite all of their extended families and friends to attend. But not Victoria's family. Why? Because she asked them not to. "I didn't want anything big," she told *Quince Años* magazine. "I really wanted to keep it low key and spend it with the people I love and trust. We ate at a really great Cuban restaurant, went to the movies and then went home and opened my gifts."

That doesn't mean Victoria didn't want to do anything for her birthday, however. "I want to go to the movies with my friends and hang out," she told *Tiger Beat* magazine. "I wanna see *He's Just Not That Into You*. But I don't know if my guy friends would be interested in seeing that with me."

So what did Victoria do for her birthday? Well, she and *Spectacular!* co-star (and good friend) Simon Curtis were signing autographs at a store. Her friends surprised her with a birthday cake, and everyone sang "Happy Birthday" to her. Victoria blew out the candles, but she didn't really need to make a wish—she'd already gotten the perfect present. A few months before, on August 13, the *Orlando Sentinel* reported that "Victoria Justice, who played Lola Martinez on *Zoey 101*, has signed a major talent deal with Nickelodeon." They went on to state: "The channel is developing a sitcom for the 15-year-old actress. The show will be set in a performing-arts school and will come from Dan Schneider, whose credits include *Zoey 101*, *iCarly* and *Drake & Josh*."

Just the day before, Victoria had confirmed the news on her website: "Hey everyone! I see someone found the press release from today's *Variety*. Yes, its true Nickelodeon is giving me my own show and yes, Sony BMG also gave me a record deal, (which is tied to the show and also as a solo artist)!!!! I'm really excited as you can probably tell from all the exclamation marks ;D. It's not a spin off, I will be a totally new character. Its kinda like my real life. Its about a girl who goes to a performing arts school, (just like I did for 3 years)."

Victoria isn't the only one who's excited. "Victoria is a rare kind of actress. She's beautiful, yet takes a fearless approach to acting," Paula Kaplan, Nickelodeon's executive vice-president, said in a press release. "Kids loved her on *Zoey 101* because she could boldly take a pie in the face or just as easily tackle a dramatic scene. It is this versatility combined with her musical talent and real-girl qualities that make her someone we are excited about."

Once it had been made official, Victoria was happy to give justjaredjr.buzznet.com a few more details. A lot of things about the show are still up in the air— including the title! "We start filming February 23," she explained to justjaredjr.buzznet.com, "and there's no character's name yet. Right now, the character's name is Vic and it's titled *The Victoria Justice Project*. But we are going to start filming it really soon, so I think [executive producer/creator] Dan Schneider will have a name soon. He's a procrastinator and always does things last minute—but they always turn out great! So maybe there's a method to that man's madness!"

At the time, Victoria didn't even know—or couldn't reveal—who would be playing some of her co-stars! "When I get back, I'm actually doing a screen test to read with the people who are auditioning," she said to justjared.buzznet.com, "which will be so much fun because I'm usually the one who has to go into the room and don't get to hear anything. So this will be cool that I'll get to hear what the network says, and what they thought of them. I always sympathize with the people that come into the room because I know how hard it is to stand up in front of ten adults and read a scene and be funny. If they laugh, that's great, but if they don't it's kind of awkward."

Victoria did know who one of her co-stars would

be, however, fifteen year-old Ariana Grande (best known for her role as Charlotte on the Broadway musical *13*) will play the role of Cat. Even if Victoria doesn't know who any of her other co-stars will be, she does know some information about the roles. She told justjaredjr.buzznet.com, "One of the other characters is 'Trina,' who is my older sister and is kind of a legend in her own mind because she thinks she is a really good singer, even though she's not that great. Then I have a best friend on the show, his name is 'Andre' and he plays the piano and is a musician. He'll be the one that I get into crazy situations with! Then there's a mean girl named 'Jade' and the James-Dean-hot-sexy guy at school named 'Beck.'"

So now Victoria Justice will have her own TV show! And wait, did she say she'd been signed for a record deal as well? Yes, she did! And she's already started work on it! "I'm also very excited about having gone into the studio last Sat.," she posted on her website on September 2, 2008. "I recorded a single. It was soo cool!! I absolutely love the song, and I think you guys will, too. I don't know when it'll be released, (we have lots of meetings coming up), but of course I'll keep u guys posted."

When justjaredjr.buzznet.com asked her if she was considering a music career at some point, Victoria said, "Music is definitely something that I want to focus on right now, too. My TV show on Nickelodeon, which I'm so excited about, is about a girl who goes to performing arts school, so it has music tied into it. So it's really cool that I get to act, sing, and dance all in my show and get to do all three things that I really love." It's exactly like that "triple threat" Simon Curtis talked about with *Spectacular!* Only this time, it's all Victoria Justice! "Victoria is the real deal," says Jay Landers, Senior VP of Columbia Records. "Besides her acting skills which are already well-known to her fans, she has a terrific recording voice. When she steps up to the mic, her personality shines through. We are looking forward to working with her and to have everyone see her in *Spectacular!* and beyond." So are we!

What else does the young star have planned? Well, she's got one major purchase in mind, though it may take her a little while yet. "I would love a car," she revealed to justjaredjr.buzznet.com, "but I don't even have my permit yet! It's really sad, I should have gotten it five months ago, but I was busy filming *Spectacular!* and then afterwards, I was supposed to study for my permit, but of course I got lazy and forgot about it. When I get back from New York, I'm totally cracking down and getting on that." She's actually practiced driving with her dad in South Carolina, since he lives in a quieter area. In fact, he probably loaned her a car, seeing as how he's the general manager at a car dealership in Rock Hill! But her mom won't let her get in the car until she has a permit. Good for you, Mom!

Victoria plans to continue her education, too. "My education is my number one priority," she told starscoop.com. "I definitely plan to go to college." Any idea where yet? "I'd really like to go to college in New York or California," she admitted to teenhollywood.com. "I'd love to take drama and theatre and still being in this field." If anyone could juggle college and a hit television and movie career, it would be Victoria—she's already managed that with middle school, high school, and even briefly with junior college! Not that it was easy. "Sometimes, it's very difficult," she told the *Hollywood Reporter.* "I get homework every night, and when you have an audition the next day, you need to work on that, too. I'm such a perfectionist that I'm always going for those straight A's, and I also want to feel that I gave the audition my all. I try to do my best at both." So far she seems to have succeeded!

So more school, more singing, and more acting. Plus, Victoria has a whole list of people she'd still love to work with. "There are too many to name," she insisted to kidzworld.com, "but let's just say for starters Meryl Streep, Hilary Swank, Johnny Depp and Mark Ruffalo. If I was thinking comedy I would have to say Steve Carell or any one of the actors from *Will and Grace.* They're all so extremely talented."

Supermodels Unlimited magazine asked Victoria what her ultimate goal was—in entertainment and in general. "To keep working and hopefully to get in the position where I can be very choosy of the projects I want to work on," Victoria answered. "I'm still really young, but I would like to have a career I can be really proud of. I love doing both drama and comedy, but my preference is probably comedy right now. I love having fun and I love to laugh. When you work with people that have great comedic timing, there's nothing better."

Well, maybe there's one thing better. That would be working with someone who's not only funny but fun, cheerful, and friendly, and both incredibly talented and just incredibly nice. Someone exactly like Victoria Justice. "I think it's so cool that some girls look up to me," she told starscoop.com. "It's a really cool thing. I just act the same as I always do. When people come up to me and ask me questions, I always try and give good advice."

Is it any wonder Victoria's career continues to impress and her star continues to rise? This girl's got unlimited potential!

CHAPTER 17
VICTORIA'S FAVES

Think you know all about Victoria? Do you own every season of *Zoey 101* on DVD? Did you buy *Gilmore Girls* season 4, just so you could watch Victoria's guest appearance over and over? Maybe you only buy GUESS jeans, just because Victoria starred in the ad campaign? Well, now it's time to put your Victoria knowledge to the test! Read on to learn some of her favorite—and least favorite—things!

FAVORITE ACTORS: James Franco, Jim Caviezel, Johnny Depp, Jamie Foxx, Robert DeNiro, Ben Stiller, and Tom Hanks

FAVORITE ACTRESSES: Juliette Lewis, Hillary Swank, and Kate Hudson

FAVORITE COMEDIAN: Steve Carell

FAVORITE MOVIES: *Almost Famous*, *The Other Sister*, *Ray*, *Meet the Parents*, *Forrest Gump*, *Million Dollar Baby*, and *Zoolander*

FAVORITE MUSICALS: *A Chorus Line*, *Bye Bye Birdie*, and *Rent*

FAVORITE MUSIC: All kinds. Her personal favorite is "pop with a little bit of rock."

FAVORITE RECORDING ARTISTS: Sara Bareilles, Alicia Keys, Pink, Usher, Madonna, Gwen Stefani, Britney Spears, Christina Aguilera, Billy Joel, Stevie Wonder, the Beatles, the Beach Boys, OutKast, and Barry Manilow

FAVORITE RAPPER: Ludacris

FAVORITE GROUP: Coldplay

FAVORITE COLDPLAY SONG: "Viva la Vida," followed closely by "Fix You" and "Yellow"

FAVORITE KARAOKE SONG: "My Girl" by the Temptations

FAVORITE TV SHOWS: *Gossip Girl*, *American Idol*, and *The Office*

FAVORITE DISNEY MOVIES: *The Little Mermaid* and *Beauty and the Beast*

FAVORITE FOODS: Cuban, Greek, and Italian

FAVORITE MEAL: Filet mignon/prime rib, cream of spinach, and a baked potato—loaded

FAVORITE FAST FOOD: Chicken Selects from McDonald's

FAVORITE DRINK: Caramel Frappucino (de-caf only) and strawberry milkshakes with extra whipped cream

FAVORITE ICE CREAM: Ben & Jerry's "Cherry Garcia" and Breyer's "Rocky Road"

FAVORITE CANDY: Sour Warheads

FAVORITE FASHION ACCESSORIES: Boots (UGGs, Western, etc.), Converse sneakers, and earrings

FAVORITE PLACES TO SHOP: Abercrombie & Fitch, Urban Outfitters, and Wet Seal

FAVORITE CLOTHING BRANDS: Juicy Couture and Abercrombie & Fitch

FAVORITE CELEBRITY FOR FASHION: Sienna Miller or Rachel Bilson

FAVORITE BEACH: Hollywood, Florida— it has a 3.5 mile boardwalk, where you can bike, rollerblade, scooter, skateboard, or whatever you're into. The water's not cold, and it's really blue green.

FAVORITE PET: Her dog Sophie, who is half bichon frise and half schnauzer. Victoria got her—and her sister Madison got her dog brother Sammy—as an early

Christmas present in December 2008.

FAVORITE SCHOOL SUBJECT: English, because Victoria loves reading, creative writing, and spelling

FAVORITE PASTIMES: Watching a great film, singing karaoke with friends, dancing (hip-hop), reading, swimming, and shopping

FAVORITE ADVICE FOR ANYONE WANTING TO BE AN ACTOR: "I would have to say," she told kidzworld.com, "that you should always keep working hard and to never give up . . . I think you should make sure you're absolutely ready before you go out on auditions. The most important thing in an audition is to feel that you gave it your best."

INTERESTS: Hanging out with friends, and family, watching movies, dancing, reading, singing karaoke, swimming, ice-skating, shopping, and singing

PET PEEVES: (These things are Victoria's NON-faves) Chapped lips, phoniness, and insensitivity to someone else's feelings. "Anyone who bullies someone, whether it's emotionally, in cyberspace, through text messaging, or physically, is not cool in my book," she told *Justine* magazine.

WEIRDEST TALENTS: "I can pick up anything with my toes, including small things like pennies," Victoria revealed to *Girl's Life* magazine. "And I can do the eyebrow wave, where I make my eyebrows move in a slow wave like the ocean. And this one is the weirdest ever. I'm really good at catching flies. My reflexes are good. I just lurk and get them."

CHAPTER 18

THE MANY SIDES OF VICTORIA JUSTICE

Victoria has so many different things she loves to do—and that she's good at! She's an actor, a singer, a dancer, and an ordinary sixteen-year-old girl! Everyone has different sides to themselves, different aspects of their personality. That's what makes you a well-rounded individual instead of a two-dimensional cut-out. What sides do you have? Do any of them match Victoria's? Let's find out!

1) It's a brand-new day, and it's time for you to hop out of bed and get moving! But where exactly are you going? Are you . . .
   - **A.** Going to the set to get into costume and makeup?
   - **B.** Heading to the studio to rehearse your latest song?
   - **C.** Off to school with your friends?

119

2) You're at your house hanging out with a bunch of your friends. There's nothing on TV and you don't want to watch anything, anyway. So what do you do for fun?

    A. Adopt roles and pretend to be movie stars?

    B. Make up silly songs about each other and other people you know?

    C. Give each other makeovers and gossip about boys?

3) Victoria Justice invites you to be her best friend for a day! The two of you will do everything together—and she leaves WHAT you do up to you! Do you . . .

    A. Ask to tour the set and meet the other actors, maybe do a walk-on yourself?

    B. Go to the studio and record a song together, and a YouTube video to go with it?

C: Chill out, go shopping, and just relax?

4) You're tense, you've had a rough day, and you need to relax. Do you . . .

    A. Pop in one of your favorite movies and lose yourself in it, reciting the lines along with the characters?

    B. Plug in your iPod and let the music carry you away, singing along?

    C. Call your friends and see if they want to hang out for a bit, even if it's just for something silly?

IF YOU CHOSE . . .

Mostly As—Your acting side has a strong hold on you. You love to play parts, and you're always watching movies, and even real people, for tips on how to fit into a role more easily. Victoria's very focused on her acting, too—it's something you have in common!

Mostly Bs—It's the music that really moves you, that speaks to your soul. You want to listen to music, and probably make music of your own. Victoria loves music as well, and in recent years has actually gotten to sing in several shows and even work on a solo album. Maybe you can, too!

Mostly Cs—For all her acting and singing, all her work and fame, Victoria's still a normal teenager at heart. And so are you! You may like acting and singing, but you'd rather hang out with your friends and have some fun. Maybe you should invite Victoria to join you!

CHAPTER 19

FINDING VICTORIA ONLINE

Want to keep up with everything that Victoria Justice is doing? It's not easy! But going online can certainly help.

The Internet is a great place to find information about all sorts of things. But remember to always ask a parent before going online, and to be careful about who you talk to when you're online. Never give your personal information—like your name, address, and phone number—to someone you don't know, or ever offer or accept an offer to meet someone in person if you've only talked to them online. You should also remember that not everything you read is true, especially on the Internet. Until you hear it directly from someone involved or from an official news source, you can't be sure information hasn't been exaggerated or completely made up.

The other thing about the Internet is how fast

it can change. The sites below are Victoria's own pages, or well-established sites and networks. There are also hundreds of Victoria Justice fansites out there, each with their own information, videos, pictures, and other details. Go ahead and browse, with your parents' permission—you may find a Victoria Justice fansite you really like. Don't worry if you can't find a site listed here—sites come and go, and new ones are popping up all the time. You might even set one up yourself!

www.victoriajustice.net

The first place to go for tons of info, obviously, is Victoria's own website! The site has a gallery, with photos from many of Victoria's projects (often behind the scenes shots of her and the rest of the cast and crew), her résumé, a news page, biography, forum, links, and contact page.

www.youtube.com/user/ victoriajustice4all

Victoria's official YouTube channel. She has warned on her blog that someone else has been pretending to be her and has put up Victoria Justice videos under the name "VictoriaJusticeMusic." The videos may be real but the identity isn't, and Victoria has asked that people avoid that person. You can go to her real YouTube channel on "victoriajustice4all" instead. Victoria has put up several short videos of her and her friends, rehearsing and singing or just goofing off.

vjustice.proboards58.com

This is Victoria's official message board. She doesn't maintain the board herself but she does visit it frequently, both to post updates in the "Victoria's Journal" section and to answer questions and chat with her fans. She also puts up links to pictures she's taken or that others have taken of her. You have to register to sign in, but registration is free and only takes a few seconds.

Unfortunately, at this point Victoria doesn't have a Facebook or MySpace page. She says that Facebook is too confusing with all the applications and games and the way the profile is set up. She likes MySpace better but hasn't found time to build her own page yet. She might someday, she admits. If she does, she'll certainly post the address on her website and her forum. Especially since there are already several MySpace pages claiming to belong to her!

You can also find information about Victoria at Wikipedia, the Internet Movie Database, and Nickelodeon.com. Between those and the sites listed above, you should be able to keep up with her latest projects. But good luck with that. Because Victoria Justice never seems to stop—she's always got several different projects in hand. And if you're like us, you'll want to see and listen to them all!